ALSO BY PHILIP LEVINE

Poetry
Breath (2004)
The Mercy (1999)
Unselected Poems (1997)
The Simple Truth (1994)
What Work Is (1991)
New Selected Poems (1991)
A Walk with Tom Jefferson (1988)
Sweet Will (1985)
Selected Poems (1984)
One for the Rose (1981)
7 Years from Somewhere (1979)
Ashes: Poems Old and New (1979)
The Names of the Lost (1976)
1933 (1974)
They Feed They Lion (1972)
Red Dust (1971)
Pili's Wall (1971)
Not This Pig (1968)
On the Edge (1963)

Essays
So Ask (2003)
The Bread of Time (1994)

Translations
Off the Map: Selected Poems of Gloria Fuertes (1984)
Edited and translated with Ada Long
Tarumba: The Selected Poems of Jaime Sabines (1979)
Edited and translated with Ernesto Trejo

Interviews
Don't Ask (1981)

NEWS OF THE WORLD

NEWS OF THE WORLD

Poems

PHILIP LEVINE

Alfred A. Knopf · New York · 2015

This Is a Borzoi Book Published by Alfred A. Knopf
Copyright © 2009 by Philip Levine

All rights reserved. Published in the United States by
Alfred A. Knopf, a division of Random House, Inc., New York,
and in Canada by Random House of Canada, Limited, Toronto.

www.aaknopf.com/poetry

Knopf, Borzoi Books, and the colophon are registered trademarks of Random House, Inc.

Library of Congress Cataloging-in-Publication Data
Levine, Philip, [date]
News of the world : poems / by Philip Levine.—1st ed.
p. cm.
ISBN 978-0-375-71190-9
I. Title.
PS3562.E9N48 2009
811'.54—dc22   2009016517

Cover photograph © Studio Patellani / Corbis
Cover design by Jason Booher

Manufactured in the United States of America

Published October 6, 2009
First Paperback Edition, February 15, 2011
Reprinted Four Times
Sixth Printing, October 2015

For Franny

CONTENTS

I

OUR VALLEY

We don't see the ocean, not ever, but in July and August
when the worst heat seems to rise from the hard clay
of this valley, you could be walking through a fig orchard
when suddenly the wind cools and for a moment
you get a whiff of salt, and in that moment you can almost
believe something is waiting beyond the Pacheco Pass,
something massive, irrational, and so powerful even
the mountains that rise east of here have no word for it.

You probably think I'm nuts saying the mountains
have no word for ocean, but if you live here
you begin to believe they know everything.
They maintain that huge silence we think of as divine,
a silence that grows in autumn when snow falls
slowly between the pines and the wind dies
to less than a whisper and you can barely catch
your breath because you're thrilled and terrified.

You have to remember this isn't your land.
It belongs to no one, like the sea you once lived beside
and thought was yours. Remember the small boats
that bobbed out as the waves rode in, and the men
who carved a living from it only to find themselves
carved down to nothing. Now you say this is home,
so go ahead, worship the mountains as they dissolve in dust,
wait on the wind, catch a scent of salt, call it our life.

UNHOLY SATURDAY

Three boys down by the river
search for crawdads. One has
hammered a spear from a
curtain rod, and head down,
jeans rolled up to his knees, wades
against the river's current.
Barely seven, he's the most
determined. He'll go home
hours from now with nothing
to show for his efforts except
dirt and sweat and that residue
he's unaware of sifting
down from a distant sky
and glinting like threads
of mica across his shoulders.
In the distance someone keeps
calling the names of the brothers
in the same order over
and over, but they don't hear
what with the riverbank gorged
with blue weed patches and all
the birds in hiding. Perhaps no
one is calling and it's only
the voices of the air as
the late light of June hangs on
in the cottonwoods before
the dark whispers the last word.

A STORY

Everyone loves a story. Let's begin with a house.
We can fill it with careful rooms and fill the rooms
with things—tables, chairs, cupboards, drawers
closed to hide tiny beds where children once slept
or big drawers that yawn open to reveal
precisely folded garments washed half to death,
unsoiled, stale, and waiting to be worn out.
There must be a kitchen, and the kitchen
must have a stove, perhaps a big iron one
with a fat black pipe that vanishes into the ceiling
to reach the sky and exhale its smells and collusions.
This was the center of whatever family life
was here, this and the sink gone yellow
around the drain where the water, dirty or pure,
ran off with no explanation, somewhat like the point
of this, the story we promised and may yet deliver.
Make no mistake, a family was here. You see
the path worn into the linoleum where the wood,
gray and certainly pine, shows through.
Father stood there in the middle of his life
to call to the heavens he imagined above the roof
must surely be listening. When no one answered
you can see where his heel came down again
and again, even though he'd been taught
never to demand. Not that life was especially cruel;
they had well water they pumped at first,
a stove that gave heat, a mother who stood
at the sink at all hours and gazed longingly
to where the woods once held the voices
of small bears—themselves a family—and the songs
of birds long fled once the deep woods surrendered
one tree at a time after the workmen arrived

with jugs of hot coffee. The worn spot on the sill
is where Mother rested her head when no one saw,
those two stained ridges were handholds
she relied on; they never let her down.
Where is she now? You think you have a right
to know everything? The children tiny enough
to inhabit cupboards, large enough to have rooms
of their own and to abandon them, the father
with his right hand raised against the sky?
If those questions are too personal, then tell us,
where are the woods? They had to have been
because the continent was clothed in trees.
We all read that in school and knew it to be true.
Yet all we see are houses, rows and rows
of houses as far as sight, and where sight vanishes
into nothing, into the new world no one has seen,
there has to be more than dust, wind-borne particles
of burning earth, the earth we lost, and nothing else.

NEW YEAR'S EVE, IN HOSPITAL

You can hate the sea as it floods
the shingle, draws back, swims up
again; it goes on night and day
all your life, and when your life
is over it's still going. A young priest
sat by my bed and asked, did I know
what Cardinal Newman said
about the sea. This merry little chap
with his round pink hands entwined
told me I should change my life.
"I like my life," I said. "Holidays
are stressful in our line of work,"
he said. Within the week he was off
to Carmel to watch the sea come on
and on and on, as Newman wrote.
"I hate the sea," I said, and I did
at that moment, the way the waves
go on and on without a care.
In silence we watched the night
spread from the corners of the room.
"You should change your life,"
he repeated. I asked had he been
reading Rilke. The man in the next bed,
a retired landscaper from Chowchilla,
let out a great groan and rolled over
to face the blank wall. I felt bad
for the little priest: both of us
he called "my sons" were failing,
slipping gracelessly from our lives
to abandon him to face eternity
as it came on and on and on.

BEFORE THE WAR

Seeing his mother coming home
he kneels behind a parked car,
one hand over his mouth to still
his breathing. She passes, climbs
the stairs, and again the street is his.
We're in an American city, Toledo,
sometime in the last century, though
it could be Buffalo or Flint,
the places are the same except
for the names. At eight or nine,
even at eleven, kids are the same,
without an identity, without a soul,
things with bad teeth and bad clothes.
We could give them names, we could
name the mother Gertrude and give her
a small office job typing bills of lading
eight hours a day, five and a half
days a week. We could give her
dreams of marriage to the boss
who's already married, but we
don't because she loathes him.
It's her son, Sol, she loves,
the one still hiding with one knee
down on the concrete drawing
the day's last heat. He's got feelings.
Young as he is, he can feel heat,
cold, pain, just as a dog would
and like a dog he'll answer
to his name. Go ahead, call him,
"Hey, Solly, Solly boy, come here!"
He doesn't bark, he doesn't sit,

he doesn't beg or extend one paw
in a gesture of submission.
He accepts his whole name, even
as a kid he stands and faces us,
just as eleven years from now
he'll stand and face his death
flaming toward him on a bridge-
head at Remagen while Gertrude
goes on typing mechanically
into the falling winter night.

MY FATHERS, THE BALTIC

Low and gray, the sky
sinks into the sea.
Along the strand stones,
busted shells, bottle tops,
dimpled beer cans.
Something began here
centuries ago,
maybe a voyage,
a nameless disaster.
Young men set out
for those continents
beyond myth
while the women
waited and the sons
grew into other men.
Looking for a sign,
maybe an amulet
against storms, I kneel
on the damp sand
to find my own face
in a small black pool,
wide-eyed, alarmed.
My grandfather crossed
this sea in '04
and never returned,
so I've come alone
to thank creation
as he would never
for carrying him home
to work, age, defeat,
those blood brothers
faithful to the end.

Yusel Prisckulnick,
I bless your laughter
thrown in the wind's face,
your gall, your rages,
your abiding love
for money and all
it never bought,
for your cracked voice
that wakens in dreams
where you rest at last,
for all the sea taught
you and you taught me:
that the waves go out
and nothing comes back.

YAKOV

My uncle told me of the cabin
in the forest, his house for years—
thirty-five or more—he'd lost count.
From miles off descending into
the valley as evening gathered
in the branches of larch and oak
he'd catch the smell of woodsmoke,
the thin plume that always brought
him home. "The silence, it was
all, it was everything."
Even the wolves, he told me, moved
through the trees without breathing.
The blackbirds vanished hours before
sunset. Snow fell only in the dark
so that at daybreak the world
was new. How he lived, what he ate,
how he dressed, who he spoke to,
what he shared, he never said.
The first sight of smoke, the silence,
the unseen wolves their tracks carved
in snow, the daily disappearances,
the sun rising, the sun failing,
the absence of another voice,
of any human voice, these were
his companions, his Siberia.
His Detroit was something else:
in the back of Automotive
a bare bulb swung above him
as he bowed to the wrong job
in the wrong place and entered
the unwritten epic of tedium,

a cigarette in one hand,
three fingers on the other.
Yakov, my old grease shop partner,
one day hung up his apron,
put down his gloves and wristbands,
and went off in smoke. If he came
to my door now on his trek
to nowhere I'd welcome him back
with black wine and black bread,
a glass of tea, a hard wood floor
to sleep on, and hope the new day
brought him the music of silence.

INNOCENCE

Smiling, my brother straddles a beer keg
outside a pub. 1944, a year
of buzz bombs. He's in the Air Corps,
on a mission to London to refill
oxygen tanks for B-24s, the flying coffins
as they were dubbed by those who flew
them night after night. Fifty years later
a German writer on a walking trip
through East Anglia meets a gardener
who recalls as a boy of twelve hearing
the planes taking off at dusk to level
the industrial cities of the Ruhr
and later when the Luftwaffe was all
but destroyed whatever they could reach.
"50,000 American lads died." The gardener
recalls waking near dawn, the planes
stuttering back in ones and twos.
How many Germans died we may
never know. "Must have been women,
children, and the very old what with
all the eligible men gone to war."
The German novelist writes it down
word for word in his mind and goes
on to an appointment with an English
writer born in Germany, a Jew
who got out in time. My brother
recalls a young woman who lived above
the pub, a blonde, snapping the picture
outside the pub with his own Argus
C3, and points out a horse and wagon
around the corner loaded with beer kegs

but with no driver. The pub is closed,
for it is not long after dawn and the city
is rising for work and war. We call the time
innocent for lack of a better word, we call
all the Germans the Nazis because it suits
the vengeance we exact. Some hours later
the two writers born in Germany sit
out in a summer garden and converse
in their adopted tongue and say nothing
about what they can't forget as children,
for these two remain children until they die.
My brother, blind now, tells me he is glad
to be alive, he calls every painful day
a gift he's not sure he earned but accepts
with joy. He lives in a Neutra house
with entire walls of glass and a view
of the Pacific, a house he bought
for a song twenty years ago in disrepair.
He accepts the fact that each year squadrons
of architectural students from Europe and Asia
drop in to view the place, and though
he cannot see he shows them around
graciously and lets them take
their photographs. When I tell him
of the 50,000 airmen the gardener told
the novelist about, his blind eyes
tear up, for above all my older brother
is a man of feeling, and his memory is precise—
like a diamond—and he says, "Not that many."

II

DEARBORN SUITE

1.

Middle-aged, supremely bored
with his wife, hating his work,
unable to sleep, he rises
from bed to pace his mansion
in slippers and robe, wondering
if this is all there ever
will be to becoming Henry Ford,
the man who created

the modern world. The skies
above the great Rouge factory
are black with coke smoke, starless,
the world is starless now, all
because he remade it in
his image, no small reward.

2.

Monday comes as it must, with a pale
moon sinking below the elms.
They told us another dawn was
on the way, possibly held up
by traffic on Grand Boulevard
or by Henry, master of Dearborn,
who loathes sharing the light
with the unenlightened among us.

That was 60 years ago.
The day arrived, a weak sun
but nonetheless an actual

one, its sooty light bathing
walls, windows, eyelids while
old pal moon drifted off to sleep.

3.

As a boy I'd known these fields
rife with wild phlox in April,
where at night the red-tailed fox
came to prey and the horned owl
split the air in a sudden rush
for its kill. I loved that world
with its little woods that held
their darkness and the still ponds,

clear as ice, that held the stars
each night until the dawn broke
into fenced plots of land,
claimed and named, barns and stables,
white houses with eyes shut tight
against the intrusion of sight.

4.

Hell is here in the forge room
where the giant presses stamp
out body parts and the smell
of burning skin seeps into
our hair and under our nails.
The old man, King Henry, punches in
for the night shift with us,
his beloved coloreds and Yids,

to work until the shattered
windows gray. There is a justice
after all, there's a bright anthem
for the occasion, something
familiar and blue, with words we
all sing, like "Time on My Hands."

AN EXTRAORDINARY MORNING

Two young men—you just might call them boys—
waiting for the Woodward streetcar to get
them downtown. Yes, they're tired, they're also
dirty and happy. Happy because they've
finished a short workweek, and if they're not rich
they're as close to rich as they'll ever be
in this town. Are they truly brothers?
You could ask the husky one, the one
in the black jacket he fills to bursting;
he seems friendly enough, snapping
his fingers while he shakes his ass and sings
"Sweet Lorraine," or if you're put off
by his mocking tone, ask the one leaning
against the locked door of Ruby's Rib Shack,
the one whose eyelids flutter in time
with nothing. Tell him it's crucial to know
if in truth this is brotherly love. He won't
get angry, he's too tired for anger,
too relieved to be here, he won't even laugh
though he'll find you silly. It's Thursday,
maybe a holy day somewhere else, maybe
the Sabbath, but these two, neither devout
nor cynical, have no idea how to worship
except by doing what they're doing,
singing a song about a woman they love
merely for her name, breathing in and out
the used and soiled air they wouldn't know
how to live without, and by filling
the twin bodies they've disguised as filth.

ARRIVAL AND DEPARTURE

Arriving in December on a Greyhound
from Paducah, you saw the usual sun
rising on your right over the bowed houses
of Dearborn as a wafer of moon descended
on your left behind the steaming rail yards
wakening for work. "Where are we?" you asked.
In 1948 people still talked
to each other even when they had something
to say, so of course I answered. I wasn't
innocent exactly, nor experienced
either, just a kid; "Downtown," I said,
as the bus with its cargo of bad breath
pulled in behind the depot just off
Washington Boulevard. Had you been
a woman, even one with crooked teeth,
a tight smile, and no particular charm,
I would have offered you a place to stay,
but at 6′ 2″ and 185
with your raw Indian features and hands
twice the size of mine, you got only advice,
in the long run not very good advice.
I should have said, "Go home, this town
will break your heart," but what did I know
about your home on a hillside tobacco farm
in North Carolina? What do I know now
except the forests as you climb higher,
dotted here and there with weathered shacks
the color of lead, and the rising silence
of winter as the snow descends unstained
into the early dusk. There was snow here, too,
speckled with cinders, piss-yellowed, tired,

and the smell of iron and ashes blowing
in from Canada, and you and I waiting
for a streetcar that finally arrived
jammed with the refuse of the night shift
at Plymouth Assembly. I should have seen
where we were headed; even at twenty
it was mine to know. Like you I thought
2.35 an hour was money, I thought
we'd sign on for afternoons and harden
into men. Wasn't that the way it worked,
men sold themselves to redeem their lives?
If there was an answer I didn't get it.
Korea broke, I took off for anywhere
living where I could, one perfect season
in your mountains. The years passed,
suddenly I was old and full of new needs.
When I went back to find you I found
instead no one in the old neighborhood
who knew who I was asking for; the Sure Shot
had become a porno shop; the plating plant
on Trumbull had moved to Mexico
or heaven. In its space someone planted
oiled grass, stripped-down cars, milkweeds
shuddering in the traffic. The river was here,
still riding low and wrinkled toward a world
we never guessed was there, but still the same,
like you, faithful to the end. If your sister,
widowed now, should call today and ask
one more time, "Where is he at? I need him,
he needs me," what should I tell her?
He's in the wind, he's under someone's
boot soles, he's in the spring grass, he lives
in us as long as we live. She won't buy it,

neither would you. You'd light a cigarette,
settle your great right hand behind my neck,
bow down forehead to forehead, your black hair
fallen across your eyes, and mutter something
consequential, "Bullshit" or "God amighty"
or "The worst is still to come." You came north
to Detroit in winter. What were you thinking?

ON ME!

In the next room his brothers are asleep,
the two still in school. They just can't wait
to grow up and be men, to make money.
Last night at dinner they sat across from him,
their brother, a man, but a man with nothing,
without money or the prospect of money.
He never pays, never tosses a bill
down on the bar so he can say, "On me!"
At four in the morning when he can't sleep,
he rehearses the stale phrase to himself
with a delicate motion of the wrist
that lets the bill float down. He can't pace
for fear of waking his mom, who sleeps
alone downstairs in the old storage room
off the kitchen. When he was a kid, twelve
or fourteen, like his brothers, he never knew
why boys no older than he did the things
they did, the robberies, gang fights, ODs,
rapes, he never understood his father's
wordless rages that would explode in punches
and kicks, bottles, plates, glasses hurled
across the kitchen. The next morning would be
so quiet that from his room upstairs
he'd hear the broomstraws scratching the floor
as his mother swept up the debris, and hear
her humming to herself. Now it's so clear,
so obvious, he wonders why it took
so long for him to get it and to come of age.

BLOOD

My brother wakens in the back room
just before dawn and hears branches
clicking against the upstairs windows.
Late summer of '45 and he's home
from a war. He's waiting for the light
to flood the room when a voice cries out,
my voice in dreams. Later that day
he and I will tramp through the fields
at the edge of town while the grass
blows around us. He won't ask
if the cry he heard was mine; instead
he'll follow me into the shaded woods
where I go evening after evening
to converse with tangled roots and vines.
Others come in pairs in winter
to breathe the frozen sky, in spring
for the perfumes of earth, girls and boys
in search of themselves. I show my brother
a tight nest of broken eggs, a fresh hole
the field mice dug. The dark begins
to collect between branches, the winds
rise until the woods moan the day's end.
We turn for home talking of plans
for the year ahead. It's still summer
though the seasons blow around us—
rain and sleet waiting in the graying air
we breathe—the future coming
toward us in the elm's black shadow,
two brothers—almost one man—
held together by what we can't share.

HOMECOMING

An actual place in the actual city
where we all grew up. You and I pass it
on the way to school or on the way home
after work. It's where the old house
once stood, its wide eyes open day and night,
replaced by nothing. Call it an empty lot
though it's not empty. Wild flags in April,
a froth of lacy white flowers Mama called
wild chicory, and milkweed, rye, broom,
in autumn the aftermath of rhubarb
no one ever harvests, a long trench
suitable for warfare and once propped
with spare timbers from the first house
that crashed here.

               Three blocks away,
where the local police station once ruled
over seventeen abandoned bungalows
and the pharmaceutical warehouse
the mice sublet, the traffic light stuck
on yellow years ago, so now the big semis
bound for Wyandotte go through
without bothering to slow. It grants
a certain misleading permissiveness
you'd expect to find in the brighter
neighborhoods of Amsterdam or Vegas,
those places where blown roses spread
their private charms on long stems
lacquered like toenails.

The real city
awakens on a late Saturday morning
in the new century to find its river
working seaward, the faceless moon—
awake all night—has stolen off
without a word. In the house
that stood here, a shade is raised
to let the day in, a woman's memory
almost takes shape as she stands
frozen at the window. If we're quiet
we might hear something alive
on the move through the dusty alleys
or the little abandoned parks, some-
thing left behind, the spirit of the place
welcoming us, if the place had a spirit.

OF LOVE AND OTHER DISASTERS

The punch press operator from up north
met the assembler from West Virginia
in a bar near the stadium. Friday, late,
but too early to go home alone. Neither
had anything in mind, so they conversed
about the upcoming baseball season
about which neither cared. We could
be a couple, he thought, but she was
all wrong, way too skinny. For years
he'd had an image of the way a woman
should look, and it wasn't her, it wasn't
anyone he'd ever known, certainly not
his ex-wife who'd moved back north
to live with her high school sweetheart.
About killed him. I don't need that shit,
he almost said aloud, and then realized
she'd been talking to someone, maybe
to him, about how she couldn't get
her hands right, how the grease ate
so deeply into her skin it became
a part of her, and she put her hand,
palm up, on the bar and pointed
with her cigarette at the deep lines
the work had carved. "The lifeline,"
he said, "which one is that?" "None,"
she said, and he noticed that her eyes
were hazel flecked with tiny spots
of gold, and then—embarrassed—looked
back at her hand which seemed tiny
and delicate, the fingers yellowed
with calluses but slender and fine.

She took a paper napkin off the bar, spit on it, and told him to hold still while she carefully lifted his glasses, leaving him half blind, and wiped something off just above his left cheekbone. "There," she said, handing him back his glasses, "I got it," and even with his glasses on, what she showed him was nothing he could see, maybe only make-believe. He thought, "Better get out of here before it's too late," but suspected too late was what he wanted.

LIBRARY DAYS

I would sit for hours with the sunlight
streaming in the high windows and know
the delivery van was safe, locked in the yard
with the brewery trucks, and my job secure.
I chose first a virgin copy of *The Idiot*
by Dostoyevsky, every page of which confirmed
life was irrational. The librarian, a woman
gone gray though young, sat by the phone
that never rang, assembling the frown
reserved exclusively for me when I entered
at 10 A.M. to stay until the light dwindled
into afternoon. No doubt her job was to guard
these treasures, for Melville was here, Balzac,
Walt Whitman, my old hero, in multiple copies
each with the aura of used tea bags. In late August
of 1951 a suited gentleman reader creaked
across the polished oaken floor to request
the newest copy of *Jane's Fighting Ships*
only to be told, "This, sir, is literature!"
in a voice of pure malice. I looked up
from the text swimming before me in hopes
of exchanging a first smile; she'd gone back
to her patient vigil over the dead black phone.
Outside I could almost hear the world, trucks
maneuvering the loading docks or clogging
the avenues and grassy boulevards of Detroit.
Other men, my former schoolmates, were off
on a distant continent in full retreat, their commands
and groans barely a whisper across the vastness
of an ocean and a mountain range. In the garden
I'd planted years before behind the old house

I'd long ago deserted, the long winter was over;
the roses exploded into smog, the African vine
stolen from the zoo strangled the tiny violets
I'd nursed each spring, the mock orange snowed
down and bore nothing, its heavy odor sham.
"Not for heaven or earth would I trade my soul,
rather would I lie down to sleep among the dead,"
Prince Myshkin mumbled on page 437,
a pure broth of madness, perhaps my part,
the sole oracular part in the final act
of the worst play ever written. I knew then
that soon I would rise up and leave the book
to go back to the great black van waiting
patiently for its load of beer kegs, sea trunks
and leather suitcases bound for the voyages
I'd never take, but first there was *War and Peace*,
there were Cossacks riding their ponies
toward a horizon of pure blood, there was Anna,
her loves and her deaths, there was Turgenev
with his impossible, histrionic squabbles,
Chekhov coughing into his final tales. The trunks—
with their childish stickers—could wait, the beer
could sit for ages in the boiling van slowly
morphing into shampoo. In the offices and shops,
out on the streets, men and women could curse
the vicious air, they could buy and sell
each other, they could beg for a cup of soup,
a sandwich and tea, some few could face life
with or without beer, they could embrace or die,
it mattered not at all to me, I had work to do.

III

FIXING THE FOOT: ON RHYTHM

For Lejan Kwint

Yesterday I heard a Dutch doctor talking to a small girl who had cut her foot, not seriously, & was very frightened by the sight of her own blood. "Nay! Nay!" he said over & over. I could hear him quite distinctly through the wall that separated us, & his voice was strong & calm, he spoke very slowly & seemed never to stop speaking; almost as though he were chanting, never too loud or too soft. Her voice, which had been explosive & shrill at first, gradually softened until I could no longer make it out as he went on talking &, I suppose, working. Then a silence, & he said, "Ah" & some words I could not understand. I imagined him stepping spryly back to survey his work. And then another voice, silent before, the girl's father, thanking him, & then the girl thanking him, now in a child's voice. A door opening & closing. And it was over.

ISLANDS

Manhattan is not an island—I don't care what you read—it's not an island. I can walk there from my house in Brooklyn, which is also not an island. You may hear that Australia is a continent. I lived there, I know it's an island, one of many in the surrounding southern oceans. For a week I stayed in a little cottage a hundred miles south of Wollongong. At low tide we would walk out onto shelves of rock & coral for miles, & I would stare out in the direction of Brooklyn & see only acres of noisily churning water & not a single person I knew. On the streets of Manhattan & Brooklyn people of all ages walk, & as they do they speak—often in private, imaginary languages—so there is a constant music. If they are alone they will speak to the pigeons & sparrows—mainland birds are a constant presence—, & if the sparrows & pigeons turn away because the talkers are sober they'll go on talking to the sunlight or the moonlight or to nothing at all. One lives inside an immense, endless opera punctuated by the high notes of sirens & the basso profundo of trucks & jackhammers & ferries & tugboats. And when you merge your own small & sincere voice with the singing you come to realize this music is merely the background to a great American epic. All these voices are singing about who you are. For a moment you are part of the mainland.

NOT WORTH THE WAIT

"Everything in Lisbon is remembered, everything is entered by hand in enormous ledgers that are preserved forever." My heart sank: I imagined myself like some sad & aged clerk out of Dickens or Melville spending day after day scanning the pages of funereal books in order to catch a name. "These people," & here he waved his hand in a circular motion that took in the dim waiter, the gray-suited man whose head was buried in a newspaper, the two passersby weighted down with enormous leather purses, "they remember the earthquake. Nothing is forgotten." "Why's that?" I said. It was simple. Nothing had happened for centuries. The navigators had all drowned. The whole country had drifted farther & farther out to sea to find its true weather, the perfect miasma in which we now sat. "Once upon a time we were Europeans," he said. His cell phone rang & rang. "You're not going to answer?" I said. No, he knew it was the colonel's wife wanting to be driven to the prison to visit her husband, who was perfectly happy working out chess problems & writing his memoirs. "If he lives long enough there will be a pardon, & the poor man will have to go free."

IN THE WHITE CITY

From up there—& he points to the bridge high above us—they tossed down the fat barber, the Falangist, to his death. "It is all in the book by the American Communist." "The Communist?" I say. Yes, the friend of Fidel Castro, Comrade Hemingway. "The tourists come because of your Mr. Hemingway, that is why *you* are here." Who can argue with this young, balding lieutenant of the Guardia Civil who has dared to leave his barracks lacking his tricorne & with only a small sidearm? In felt house slippers he stands at ease on the wet streets of his town, Ronda, to show me the world. "On those rocks," he continues, pointing to a ledge halfway down the gorge, "he first hits & his belly explodes. Then they rape his beautiful daughter, the film star that is Swedish, & when they have finish they shave her head. That is why we execute them all." Does he mean that is why in the novel the Nationalists executed them? (I am careful not to say "the fascists"; it is 1965.) "No, no, executed them here, in life or death"—he smiles at his little joke— "up there on the bridge"—& he points again,—"by military firing squad one at a time, properly. That is why the whole town must witness & learn. It is educational." But, I insist, the death of the Falangist was merely in a novel that made no effort to be true to events, *una novela*, a fiction, a best seller. The lieutenant enjoys this repartee, he's amused by my innocence, he shakes his head, he is discreet & patient with this visitor to his ancient city that boasts the first Plaza de Toros in all the world. "You Americans," & he suppresses his laughter, "you think because he was a famous red he could not tell the truth. They do not give Noble Prizes to liars."

OLD WORLD

On the train from Copenhagen to Helsingør a tiny, deformed
woman jerked on my sleeve until I stopped reading & looked up.
"You will see there ahead the Royal Deer Park," & she pointed over
my shoulder to the manicured acres of startling green that
streamed by. Her cheeks, though powdered & rouged, looked dry
as parchment; even her little darting tongue seemed too red, made
up. "In your land you have not this?" she asked. Speaking slowly—
still caught up in my novel—I explained that in my country we
had no kings or queens and therefore no royal parks. "Exactly," she
said, & her white-gloved hand abruptly closed my book. "Here in
my kingdom you must not read, you must look."

CLOSED

The diner was closed. The two brothers stared through the window & could see no one behind the counter. One small light burned over the cash register, but not even the yellow tiger cat that adorned the counter was home today. Max, the huskier brother in a checked mackinaw, suggested they find another dump. "If Teresa's ain't open, nothing gonna be open," Bernie, his taller, wiry brother said. "There's the Greek," said Max, "come on, it's close." The Greek was actually Yervan, an Armenian who'd opened a small grocery store that sold delicatessen across from the transmission plant. Bernie thought of lighting a joint on the short walk but realized he was too tired for that. "What you got today, Nick?" Max said. "What you want?" said the Greek. "Coffee & two eggs over easy with crisp bacon & whole wheat toast," said Bernie. Yervan told them to try Teresa's because this wasn't a restaurant. "You call Teresa's a restaurant?" said Max. "For eight hours I been thinking of nothing but breakfast," said Bernie. "This has spoiled my whole weekend, maybe my whole life." By this time the sun had cleared the stacks of the transmission plant & broken through the dusty window of the deli. The Greek shielded his eyes & knew it was going to be a long day; maybe he'd clean the front window, tidy up the place. "I got coffees & fresh milks," he said, "those little pies you guys like." "Okay," said Bernie & put both hands on the counter & leaned in to them. "If I had anything left in me," he said, "I'd cry."

THE LANGUAGE PROBLEM

Cuban Spanish is incomprehensible even to Cubans. "If you spit in his face he'll tell you it's raining," the cabdriver said. In Cuban it means, "Your cigar is from Tampa." Single, desperate, almost forty, my ex-wife told the Cuban doctor she'd give a million dollars for a perfect pair of tits. "God hates a coward," he said, & directed her to an orthopedic shoe store where everything smelled like iodine. A full-page ad on the back of *Nueva Prensa Cubana* clearly read "Free rum 24 hours a day & more on weekends." ("Free rum" was in italics.) When I showed up that evening at the right address, Calle Obispo, 28, the little merchant I spoke to said, "Rum? This is not a distillery." They were flogging Venetian blue umbrellas for $4 American. Mine was made in Taiwan and when it rained refused to open. Before sunset the streets filled with music. In the great Plaza de la Revolución the dark came slowly, filled with the perfume of automobile exhaust and wisteria. I danced with a girl from Santiago de Cuba. Gabriela Mistral García was her name; she was taller than I & wore her black hair in a wiry tangle. She was a year from her doctorate in critical theory. After our dance she grabbed me powerfully by the shoulders as a *comandante* in a movie might, leaned down as though to kiss me on the cheek, & whispered in my good ear, "I dream of tenure." It was the fifties all over again.

NEWS OF THE WORLD

Once we were out of Barcelona the road climbed past small farm-houses hunched down on the gray, chalky hillsides. The last person we saw was a girl in her late teens in a black dress & gray apron carrying a chicken upside down by the claws. She looked up & smiled. An hour later the land opened into enormous green mead-ows. At the frontier a cop asked in guttural Spanish almost as bad as mine why were we going to Andorra. "Tourism," I said. Laugh-ing, he waved us through. The rock walls of the valley were so abrupt the town was only a single street wide. Blue plumes of smoke ascended straight into the darkening sky. The next morning we found what we'd come for: the perfect radio, French-made, portable, lightweight, slightly garish with its colored dial & chromed knobs, inexpensive. "Because of the mountains, reception is poor," the shop owner said, so he tuned in the local Communist station beamed to Spain. "Communist?" I said. Oh yes, they'd come twenty-five years ago to escape the Germans, & they'd stayed. "Back then," he said, "we were all reds." "And now?" I said. Now he could sell me anything I wanted. "Anything?" He nodded. A tall, graying man, his face carved down to its essentials. "A Cadil-lac?" I said. Yes, of course, he could get on the phone & have it out front—he checked his pocket watch—by four in the afternoon. "An American film star?" One hand on his unshaved cheek, he gazed upward at the dark beamed ceiling. "That could take a week."

IV

ALBA

On bad springs bouncing and swaying down
the coast road south of the city to a spit
of land overlooking the sea, they trucked
the merchant princes and their courtiers
in their gunmetal suits and soured white shirts.
Portly, substantial men, manufacturers
of camshafts, holiday bunting, antacids,
dispensers of bifocals and mornings
of benzene mists, architects of newspapers and
cardboard communes stuttering up the slopes
of Montjuich. Prodded, they limped, shoeless,
over the rocky ground to where the land
stopped at last and the waves broke far below,
deafening the air, and waited, some hopeful,
smoking, some silent, some whispering, a few
kneeling alone, praying, while the militiamen
squatted facing them, their heads falling
in and out of sleep. The warm wind
—the one they call the Levante—that blew
in the first scraps of dawn from Africa
churned the waves below from black to cobalt.
All at once the men were herded
to the land's edge and shot dead. I'm told
on good authority there is a lesson here,
one I am in need of. For González Brilla,
twenty-five, the militia commandant,
his head wrapped in a red and black scarf,
the lesson was clear. Before the ragged volley
called in the day, he shouted it out,
but with the wind swirling, the waves breaking
and those about to die abusing their gods,

no one heard. (Within a year Brilla himself,
bound and gagged in a damp cellar
off Calle Montcado, was shot just once
above his unfurrowed nape, and left
no written record.) On the ride back
to Barcelona it is reported—and now in print—
he told the driver that the air of Spain
was clearer now, although both men stank
of cordite. Years later his comrade,
Ramón Puig, told the English historian
that the night before the executions—
while oiling his Astra 9mm
taken from the body of a Guardia officer—
Brilla had rehearsed his speech:
"You, the guilty, who are about to die,
to leave the stage of history, behold . . .
behold . . . something or other" was all
Puig could ever remember. The widow,
Mercedes Brilla Robles, swears he never spoke
that way in his whole life. White-haired, shrunk
to almost nothing, she lives on state welfare
plus foreign contributions in a village
south of Perpignan. Her Spanish
is ragged now, her Catalan and French
perfect as she speaks of her girlhood days
as an anarchist rebel, the urban communes,
the battle for the telephone exchange,
the government betrayals, the journey
of the defeated on foot across the mountains
in February of '39, the iron hunger
in the French camps, the terrible war
that followed, even her years as a hairdresser.
Unfortunately she can go on forever.

I know. When by accident I found Ramón Puig
three weeks ago in a ward of the tiny
public hospital in Santa Coloma
de Gramenet he remembered nothing,
not even the war, the people armed,
the glory days of '36, and what came after,
much less Brilla's words. Then by pure luck,
seventeen kilometers south of Castelldelfels,
this bright spring morning, we found the place
where the road—impossibly narrow and steep—
hugs the coastline as it twists and climbs
until a brief widening appears.
My wife and I stopped and parked the rental car.
Hand in hand we walked to the edge
of the continent. No gunfire echoed
from the past, or if it did, the sea
silenced it. To the south, Sitges
with its fake Irish pubs and swanky new hotels,
to the north Barcelona barely visible
in its familiar, rosy shroud, dead ahead
the ancient impossible sea moving
slowly toward us as it broods on itself.
Can we hear them now, the words of Brilla,
the elusive lesson worth all those lives?
Above the cries of seagulls, the message comes
translated into the language of water and wind,
decipherable, exact, unforgettable, the same
words we spoke before we spoke in words.

THE MUSIC OF TIME

The young woman sewing
by the window hums a song
I don't know; I hear only
a few bars, and when the trucks
barrel down the broken street
the music is lost. Before the darkness
leaks from the shadows of
the great cathedral, I see her
once more at work and later
hear in the sudden silence
of nightfall wordless music rising
from her room. I put aside
my papers, wash, and dress
to eat at one of the seafood
places along the great avenues
near the port where later
the homeless will sleep. Then I
walk for hours in the Barrio
Chino passing the open
doors of tiny bars and caves
from which the voices of old men
bark out the stale anthems
of love's defeat. "This is the world,"
I think, "this is what I came
in search of years ago." Now I
can go back to my single room,
I can lie awake in the dark
rehearsing all the trivial events
of the day ahead, a day that begins

when the sun clears the dark spires
of someone's god, and I waken
in a flood of dust rising from
nowhere and from nowhere comes
the actual voice of someone else.

DURING THE WAR

When my brother came home from war
he carried his left arm in a black sling
but assured us most of it was still there.
Spring was late, the trees forgot to leaf out.

I stood in a long line waiting for bread.
The woman behind me said it was shameless,
someone as strong as I still home, still intact
while her Michael was burning to death.

Yes, she could feel the fire, could smell
his pain all the way from Tarawa—
or was it Midway?—and he so young,
younger than I who was only fourteen,

taller, more handsome in his white uniform
turning slowly gray the way unprimed wood
grays slowly in the grate when the flames
sputter and die. "I think I'm going mad,"

she said when I turned to face her. She placed
both hands on my shoulders, kissed each eyelid,
hugged me to her breasts, and whispered wetly
in my bad ear words I'd never heard before.

When I got home my brother ate the bread
carefully one slice at a time until nothing
was left but a blank plate. "Did you see her,"
he asked, "the woman in hell, Michael's wife?"

That afternoon I walked the crowded streets
looking for something I couldn't name,
something familiar, a face or a voice or less,
but not these shards of ash that fell from heaven.

THE DEATH OF MAYAKOVSKY

Philadelphia, the historic downtown,
April 14, 1930.
My father sits down at the little desk
in his hotel room overlooking an airshaft
to begin a letter home: "Dear Essie,"
he pens, but the phone rings before he can
unburden his heart. The driver from Precision Inc.
has arrived. Alone in the backseat, hatless,
coatless, on this perfect spring day,
my father goes off to inspect aircraft bearings
that vanished from an army proving ground
in Maryland, bearings he will bargain for
and purchase in ignorance, or so he will tell Essie,
my mother, this after he takes a plea
in the federal courthouse in downtown Detroit.
I knew all this before it happened. Earlier that
morning storm clouds scuttled in across Ontario
to release their darkness into our gray river.
Hundreds of miles east my father rolls down
the car window; the air scented with leaves
just budding out along Route 76
caresses his face and tangles his dark hair.
He lets the world come to him, even this world
of small machine shops, car barns, warehouses
beside the Schuylkill. The child I would become
saw it all, yet years passed before the scene slipped,
frozen, into the book of origins to become
who I am. I'd been distracted
in the breathless dawn by a single shot—
the Russian poet's suicidal gesture—
that would crown our narratives, yours and mine.

TWO VOICES

I heard a voice behind me in the street
calling my name. This was not years ago,
this was yesterday in Brooklyn, late spring
of the new year, the flowers—roses, tulips,
mock oranges, pansies—shouting their colors
along the promenade. I was on my way
to nothing, just ambling along, my head
altogether empty on a Saturday morning
in my seventy-third year. Not altogether empty,
for the flowers were in it, and the crowds
of kids in bright shirts and sweaters, young kids
with their parents in tow, and across the river
there was the city breaking through the haze
to call to the Heights, to belittle Brooklyn
as it always does. Then my name, "Philip,"
a huge voice, deep and resonant, unfamiliar
or if heard before heard on radio or TV,
too sonorous for daily life. So, of course,
I turned to behold more kids on Rollerblades,
kids on skateboards, kids on foot, no one
especially aware of me. Waiting, awake now
as I had not been, certain the morning meant
more than I'd come looking for. The crowds
passed, the sun grew stronger, the day passed
into afternoon and I gave up at last and turned
for home half-believing I'd missed something.
Let's say I phone you tonight and tell you
my little adventure which came to nothing.
What will you think? Not what will you say,
you'll say it was an illusion or you'll say
there was a deep need in me to hear
that particular voice, or sometimes the voices

of the air—all the separate voices in so
public a place—can unite for a moment
to produce "Philip" or "John" or "Robert"
or whatever we expect. I don't know
what you'll think, I've never known, even
when you and I were together, and I'd
waken in the false dawn to hear you
in the secret voice that was yours crying
out into the dark a name not mine.

THE HEART OF OCTOBER

Dusk south of Barcelona, the slopes
leading up to the fortress, a city
of wooden crates and cardboard shacks
staggers up the mountain as the rain
runs down, a black river. The final night,
I whisper to no one. A patch of red,
the single moving thing, comes toward me
to become the shirt of a young girl,
eleven or twelve. Bare-legged, picking
her way to avoid the sharp stones,
she reaches me. Through perfect teeth
in her perfect mouth she demands a *duro*,
one hand held out. Only one *duro*,
she insists, stamping a naked foot,
browned and filthy on the filthy earth.
When I pay up and turn for home
she is beside me laughing as the rain
streams down her forehead, her short hair
a black cap plastered in place. "A *duro!*"
she demands again. "Another?" I say.
"Yes, of course," she laughs into the face
of the rain, "and after that another."
Even a child knows the meaning of rain:
it is the gift of October, a gift
that arrives on time each autumn
to darken the makeshift shacks and lighten
the hillside with a single splash of color.

BURIAL RITES

Even on a rare morning of rain,
like this morning, with the low sky
hoarding its riches except for
a few mock tears, the hard ground
accepts nothing. Six years ago
I buried my mother's ashes
beside a young lilac that's now
taller than I, and stuck the stub
of a rosebush into her dirt
where, like everything else not
human, it thrives. The small blossoms
never unfurl; whatever they know
they keep to themselves until
a morning rain or a night wind
pares the petals down to nothing.
Even the neighbor cat who shits
daily on the paths and then hides
deep in the jungle of the weeds
refuses to purr. It's right to end up
beside the woman who bore me,
to shovel into the dirt whatever's left
and leave only a name for some-
one who wants it. Think of it,
my name, no longer a portion
of me, no longer inflated
or bruised, no longer stewing
in a rich compost of memory
or the simpler one of bone, kitty-
litter, the roots of the eucalyptus
I planted back in '73,
a tiny me taking nothing, giving
nothing, empty, and free at last.

MAGIC

The Michigan Central Terminal
—now only a hollow shell surrounded
by double chain-link fences and ignored—
was once the scene of my enlightenment.
At sixteen, still blond, still Nordic, I walked
the blue-blooded pets sprung from their cages:
mainly emaciated borzois
bound for Florida or California,
though now and then a baby Bengal prized
by the Dodge brothers of automobile fame.
Later I graduated to watering the elephants,
tiny ones from distant zoos or circuses
who showed such patience and understanding
with my ineptitude. When I grew into
myself, squat and bull-necked, I worked
the long afternoon shifts unloading boxcars
crammed with the treasures of a world
I'd never dreamed: from France an elixir
called "Penrod" in elaborate bottles
studded with medals and calling forth
memories of stolen dime-store moments,
a cardboard carton that terrified us all,
weightless, scored with skull and crossbones,
marked RADIUM in letters a foot high.
We placed it alone on a wooden trundle
and stood back, awed, as before a holy relic.
One midnight my newfound companions
introduced me to the common miracle
of Seven Crown and cherry schnapps with beer
for chasers and burgers fried in pork fat—
four for a dollar—served in Spud's café.

Some of the Irish and Albanians
liked to fight, especially on Friday nights
after our shift. My friend Carey, who loved
the music of Lester Young, told me one night
if I cared to take part I was welcome.
I felt honored. At the appointed hour
behind the bar across from the terminal
we waited for the Germans from Downriver,
while Carey beat out the rhythm to "Lester Leaps"
with his black cracked boots called "stompers."
He was so happy, so much the total Carey,
chanting "This is my night" to a hazy sky.
I could see semis gearing down on Fort Street,
but not the familiar stars, icy and pure
in the black sky of April 1950,
loyal companions throughout my childhood.
Though Carey raged, the Germans never showed,
a loss we took personally as a betrayal
worthy of a Judas, a verdict against creation.
Never again would the moon and stars converse
with a solitary soul trudging home
on Fridays filled with the knowledge a week
had ended changing nothing. When I tell
my grandkids I grew up in a magic world
in which cats and dogs traveled first class,
snow arrived as late as June to cool
the switch engines, and elms and maples
sprang up full-grown overnight between the tracks
and held their leaves through a dozen seasons,
they wink at each other and pretend I'm sane.
I never mention Carey or his friend,
the Mexican middleweight who hit me
for saying you could spell Catholic without

a capital "C." Although I'd known facts were useless,
something essential vanished from my world
when Carey joined the air force, the county
cut down the last family of copper beeches
to make way for US 24, and the full moon
turned its back on me for the duration.
Two years later, Carey, back from Korea
with graying hair and a flying cross,
smashed his old 78s of Pres cut
before World War II, the high tenor cry
behind Billie Holiday that took us closer to paradise
than we'd ever been. It took me years to learn
a way of walking under an umbrella
of indifferent stars, and to call them "heavenly
bodies," to regard myself as no part
of a great scheme that included everything.
I had to put one foot in front of another,
hold both arms out for balance, stare ahead,
breathe like a beginner, and hope to arrive.

NOTES

Page 14, "Innocence":
The poem owes a great deal to W. G. Sebald's depiction in *The Rings of Saturn* of a walking trip he took in East Anglia. In the poem the novelist is on the way to see the German-born English poet and translator Michael Hamburger.

Page 32, "Library Days":
The phrase "my former schoolmates . . . off on a distant continent" is a reference to those drafted into the service during the Korean War.

Page 39, "Not Worth the Wait":
One of the military leaders of the coup that brought down Salazar's forty-year dictatorship in Portugal was later charged with being a member of a terrorist organization, and though popularly known as "the father of Portuguese democracy," he was sentenced to seventeen years in prison.

Page 57, "The Heart of October":
The mountain in the poem is Montjuich, just south of Barcelona. A *duro* was a five-peseta coin, worth less than a dime in 1965.

Page 59, "Magic":
"Pernod" is deliberately misspelled ("Penrod") to capture the pronunciation of a friend. "Pres" is short for "president" and was the nickname Billie Holiday bestowed upon Lester Young. It stuck.

ACKNOWLEDGMENTS

My thanks to the editors of the following publications
in which these poems first appeared:

Arundel: "Blood"
Five Points: "A Story," "Islands," "Not Worth the Wait,"
    "Old World," "Alba"
The Georgia Review: "Innocence," "Library Days,"
    "The Heart of October"
The Kenyon Review: "The Death of Mayakovsky"
The Massachusetts Review: "Yakov"
Michigan Quarterly Review: "The Language Problem"
The New Yorker: "Before the War," "Dearborn Suite,"
    "On Me!" "Homecoming," "Of Love and Other Disasters,"
    "During the War," "Burial Rites," "Two Voices"
The Normal School: "In the White City"
The Ohio Review: "Fixing the Foot: On Rhythm"
Ploughshares: "My Fathers, the Baltic," "Arrival and Departure"
Poetry: "New Year's Eve, in Hospital," "Our Valley,"
    "An Extraordinary Morning"
Rattle: "The Music of Time"
The Southern Review: "Closed"
The Threepenny Review: "Unholy Saturday,"
    "News of the World," "Magic"

"News of the World," "Fixing the Foot: On Rhythm," "Old
World," "Closed," "Not Worth the Wait," "Islands," and "The
Language Problem" appeared in the chapbook *The Language Problem,*
Aureole Press, Toledo, 2008.

My thanks to the Rockefeller Foundation and especially to the
staff and fellow residents of the Bellagio Study and Conference
Center, where this book was completed.

My thanks to Tom Sleigh, Ed Hirsch, Peter Everwine, and my wife,
Franny, all of whom read the manuscript and suggested changes.

A NOTE ABOUT THE AUTHOR

Philip Levine was born in 1928 in Detroit and was formally educated there, in the public schools and at Wayne University (now Wayne State University). After a succession of industrial jobs, he left the city for good and lived in various parts of the country before settling in Fresno, California, where he taught at the state university until his retirement. Afterward he taught at several other colleges and universities including Tufts, Princeton, Columbia, the University of California at Berkeley, and Brown. For many years he was poet-in-residence at New York University. He received many awards for his books of poems, including two National Book Awards for *Ashes* and *What Work Is,* and the Pulitzer Prize in 1995 for *The Simple Truth.* He was a chancellor of the Academy of American Poets and Poet Laureate of the United States (2011–2012). In later years, he divided his time between Fresno, California, and Brooklyn, New York. He died shortly after his eighty-seventh birthday on February 14, 2015.

A NOTE ON THE TYPE

The text of this book was set in Centaur, the only typeface designed by Bruce Rogers (1870–1957), the well-known American book designer. A celebrated penman, Rogers based his design on the roman face cut by Nicolas Jenson in 1470 for his Eusebius. Jenson's roman surpassed all of its forerunners and even today, in modern recuttings, remains one of the most popular and attractive of all typefaces.

The italic used to accompany Centaur is Arrighi, designed by another American, Frederic Warde, and based on the chancery face used by Lodovico degli Arrighi in 1524.

COMPOSED BY
North Market Street Graphics, Lancaster, Pennsylvania

PRINTED AND BOUND BY
Thomson-Shore, Dexter, Michigan

DESIGNED BY
Iris Weinstein